Morocco

by Julie Murray

Abdo Kids Jumbo is an Imprint of Abdo Kids
abdobooks.com

abdobooks.com

Published by Abdo Kids, a division of ABDO, P.O. Box 398166, Minneapolis, Minnesota 55439.

Abdo Kids Jumbo™ is a trademark and logo of Abdo Kids.

Printed in the United States of America, North Mankato, Minnesota.

052024

092024

Photo Credits: Alamy, Getty Images, Shutterstock, ©Ian p7 / CC BY-SA 4.0

Production Contributors: Teddy Borth, Jennie Forsberg, Grace Hansen
Design Contributors: Laura Graphenteen, Candice Keimig

Library of Congress Control Number: 2023948677

Publisher's Cataloging-in-Publication Data

Names: Murray, Julie, author.

Title: Morocco / by Julie Murray

Description: Minneapolis, Minnesota : Abdo Kids, 2025 | Series: Countries | Includes online resources and index.

Identifiers: ISBN 9798384900719 (lib. bdg.) | ISBN 9798384901419 (ebook) | ISBN 9798384901761 (Read-to-me eBook)

Subjects: LCSH: Morocco--History--Juvenile literature. | Africa--Juvenile literature. | Africa--History—Juvenile literature. | Morocco--Social life and customs--Juvenile literature. | Geography--Juvenile literature. | Foreign countries --Juvenile literature.

Classification: DDC 964.0--dc23

Table of Contents

Morocco

Morocco is a country in northwest Africa. It borders two countries by land. Two bodies of water also border the country. More than 37 million people live there.

Europe

Atlantic Ocean

Spain

Strait of Gibraltar

Alboran Sea

Morocco

Algeria

Western Sahara

Africa

History

The first Moroccan state was founded in 788 CE. It has been ruled by many **dynasties** over the years.

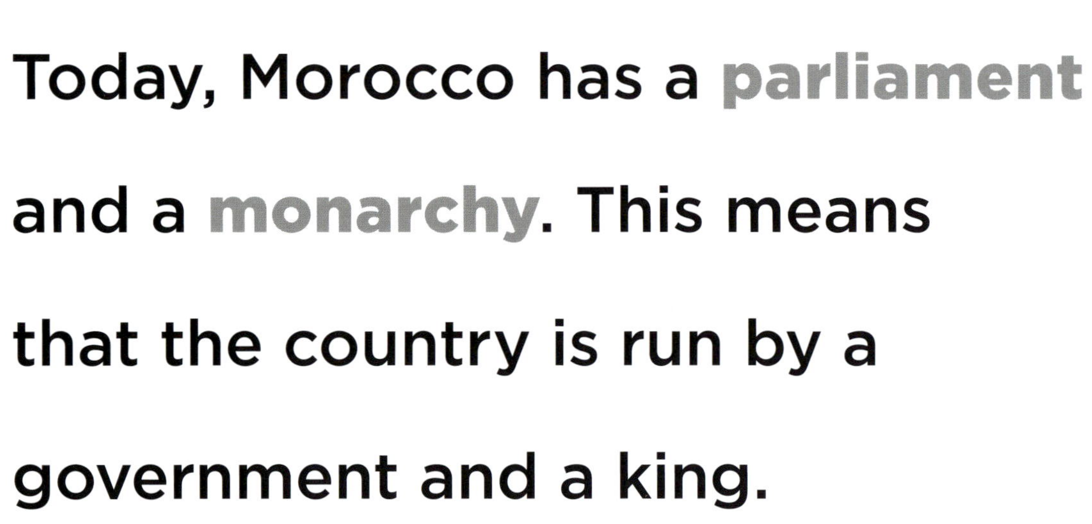

Today, Morocco has a **parliament** and a **monarchy**. This means that the country is run by a government and a king.

The Royal Palace
Fes, Morocco

Cities

Rabat is the capital of Morocco. The city is rich in history and **culture**. Rabat has beautiful buildings and many parks and gardens.

Rabat
Morocco

Casablanca is the largest city in Morocco. More than 3.3 million people live there. It is the main **port** and business center of the country.

Casablanca
Morocco

Marrakesh is known as the "Red City." Its buildings are red and glow in the sun. Marrakesh is famous for its souks. These marketplaces are full of goods!

Morocco
Marrakesh
LE SOUK PRINCIPAL DE TAPIS
LA VENTE AUX ENCHERES
THE PRINCIPAL MARKET OF CARPETS

Food

Beans, peas, and **lentils** are eaten regularly in Morocco. Spices and flower buds are often added to food. Lamb and chicken are popular meats. Sweet tea is enjoyed daily.

The Land

Morocco has mountains, plains, and deserts. Two mountain ranges run through the country. Wide plains lie in the middle. These provide rich farming land.

The Sahara Desert is the largest desert in the world. It runs along the eastern and southern borders of Morocco. The Sahara has little rainfall and high temperatures. Only special animals can survive there.

Moroccan spiny-tailed lizard
Arabian camel
fennec fox

Awesome Landmarks

Chefchaouen
Chefchaouen, Morocco

Jemaa el-Fnaa
Marrakesh, Morocco

Rif Mountains
Northern Morocco

Sahara Desert Dunes
Southern Morocco

Glossary

culture – the language, customs, ideas, and art of a particular group of people.

dynasty – a series of rulers from the same family or group.

lentil – a round, flat seed produced by the lentil plant. It is used as food.

monarchy – government by or in the name of a king, queen, or similar ruler, whose power may be strong or limited.

parliament – a group of people who make the laws for a country.

port – a place where ships load and unload, and its nearby town or city.

Index

Visit **abdokids.com** to access crafts, games, videos, and more!

Use Abdo Kids code

CMK0719

or scan this QR code!